VARANASI WITHIN VARANASI

VARANASI WITHIN VARANASI

poems

Sharmila Ray

CLASSIX

New Delhi | Calcutta

Published by CLASSIX (an imprint of *Hawakal*)

70 B/9 Amritpuri, East of Kailash, New Delhi 110065
33/1/2, K B Sarani, Mall Road, Kolkata 700080, India

info@hawakal.com
www.hawakal.com

First edition November 2022

Cover photograph by Plabon Das

Cover designed by Bitan Chakraborty

Typeset in Adobe Garamond Pro (12 pts)

Printed & bound in Thomson Press (India) Ltd, New Delhi 110020

ISBN: 978-93-91431-80-8 (Paperback)

USD 14.99

for
Sri Shama Churn Lahiree
and
Ma

...my universe...

Varanasi And I

In my imagination, Varanasi always appears as a colour maze. A city close to my heart, a place I return to again and again. Here life is scattered on the steps of the ghats, under huge umbrellas, lanes, and by-lanes. Here I believe the gods come down, their arms outstretched, embracing all, and the grass grows from the skin of the stone steps leading to the river Ganga. For me, Varanasi is elusive, ephemeral, also warm, and embracing if you want to be embraced by the city.

Varanasi is a massive painting across time where stories, legends, and facts gather to rot, to give birth to complete and incomplete stories inviting the spectator to weave their own narrative. Novelty, surprise, and the unreal all contribute to the making of the city. Wretched at one point and tantalizing, seductive at the other. I wonder if enigmas are meant to be like this; Varanasi is an enigma.

Sharmila Ray
November 2022
Calcutta

Varanasi was not built in a day.
It started in one ochre afternoon—
Palaces, ghats, temples...
globules of bliss
created, perhaps, by a sleeping god.

In Varanasi if you care to lift the veil from
your eyes, the earth becomes a pale blue dot
floating in the dark vastness of the universe
and you are reduced to atoms coming into being
from the deep depths of far-away stars.

You cannot avoid smell in Varanasi
not a superstore fragrance of Lavender and Vanilla.
Hibiscus, Marigold, milk and dust—
An aroma-permit to intoxication.

Flight of stone steps descend to the Ganga,
or if you like ascend to the city,
their surface uneven, eroded by footsteps...
Each an archive of human life rooted deep,
under the molten gold of midday heat.

The Ganga creates ripples in the water,
each a step to the horizon.
Dusk floats on the river...
I bend down to pick up happiness.

Once if you are embraced by the city
your vision takes a three hundred and sixty degrees turn.
You are enthralled, ensnared in it,
you leave only to return.

Narrow alley-ways, steaming earthenware cups of tea,
sounds of ajan and bhajan...
A small universe chiseled out from a larger script—
You swathe yourself in alphabets
there is no other way.

Moon-eyed I sit on a wayside bench,
a builder tramples dry leaves, a paper kite flies.
My morning tea steaming...
Deep-past gushes out of an ancient slab stone.

Memories are timeless,
condemned to sprout in our minds—
Varanasi waters the roots
and you are caught in a double-sided mirror.

Look at the Ganga from a high vantage point
a river that carries you far away—
Down below the boats and bathers are minuscule dots.
We are anonymous.

In Varanasi only death is not death
but moksha
and ash is not grey
but the colours of dawn.

Bordered by ghats and umbrellas huge,
here, the Ganga is an unending story.
I have traced it on my mind and
kept it close to me as an unwritten volume.

A small incision in the water;
A oar of a boat steering it towards the ghat.
Afternoon washes the landscapes with an opium-mustard tint.
But caws of a crow smashes the stillness.

Every heart is a soft shore in Varanasi
porous enough to resonate other hearts
and in the distance the river seems like a sandstone block
engraved with silence and solitude.

Between the covers of the sky and earth lie Varanasi,
I tried to gather its ancestry into an octavo volume.
Failed miserably, for what was memory was infinite,
I couldn't find equivalent words for it.

Discovering the layers of time one by one,
witnessing conversation and fragmentary dialogue,
Varanasi will surely intoxicate you
between jingling of bells and twilight.

Midday heat in the city sizzles
sucking moisture from the air—
Indoor, people sweat in T-shirts
waiting for the evening Ganga-boon.

It's raining in Varanasi
I've just come back from the Ganga ghat.
Rains scatter, fall and penetrate the city-bottom,
while my thoughts float on the surface.

Long heavy downpour and
the narrow lanes are flooded.
Hardly you see anybody outside. Just
then you catch a glimpse of a Marigold garland
floating, unattached.

In the monsoon, Varanasi is cool mud-splashed,
the Durga Temple floor turns slippery.
Pilgrims'feet bring rain water and the lamps
create golden zigzag out of it.

In the Durga Temple the monkeys fold hands
on their chest just like us.
Perhaps, they pray to goddess Durga.
We bargain with her with offerings.

Every city has a smell.
Varanasi is camphor and incense,
an offering to gods.
And the gods come down to the ghats
among saints and sinners and every
eager couple in love.

Splashing colours of a midday sun
splinters the landscape of Varanasi,
exiled on earth this perfect heaven,
its tongue cleaving the roof of your mouth.

In the cool of the evening, shadows follow me
from lane to lane—sharp, blunt, diffused...
Till they get lost in unnavigable darkness.

Have you observed the stone steps of the ghats
scratched, worn thin and sometimes with
tufts of grass sprouting?
Each has a narrative of its own
if you care to decode it.

Evening has never seemed so warm and dazzling
flame from oil lamps creating lace of lights.
I sit on the steps of the ghat lost in thought,
someone is tearing off my dark cloak.

Ganga flows, with it history.
But sometimes I think people have mopped everything clean
with their smirking-hate.
But the Ganga flows, the sky and stars her witness.

From brick to brick, stone to stone, Varanasi watches you.
If you are fortunate
Grace wraps you in silence and love
so that you put everything in their proper places before
closing your eyelids.

Gaudy calicoes float with the occasional breeze
from chaliced balconies and the city swells
in the afternoon haze to touch the ancient footsteps
of Bimbisara which echoes subterranean.

Ganga, the ghats, a drop of a solemn tear,
whispering secrets displacing time,
Varanasi the unwritten poem waits,
silent beneath a starry sky.

Have you ever felt that Varanasi is a single piece of music?
Denied by our senses, it lies
hidden in the half-light of our crowded mind.
Remove the draperies and bric-a-brac
and you will find the melody
to tune yourself.

How many shades of history are embedded in Varanasi?
Only the moon and fish know.
Just give me your hand and walk on.
Perhaps, a ripple in the Ganga will answer you.

I flipped the pages of history, legend and tradition
and found Varanasi cuddled-up in all of them,
Varanasi still lingers,
dragging me backward,
a city blooming where eternity traverses the earth.

Varanasi has a small gate unlatched
situated in the jigsaw puzzle of now,
if you are fortunate and can enter through the gate
Shiva winnows the sand of your heart.

I get up close a window, it's past midnight.
The translucent lampshade in the corner of the room
creates a blurring effect.
I sense stories of primeval Varanasi,
they spin, fall in the gap between my room
and the uninhabited byways of sleep.

Have you ever closed your eyes
and sat still forgetting you are you?
Then the morning enters you,
your eyes open and you learn to see.

Some visit temples others sit on the waterfront,
infidels and saints anoint Varanasi with their sap.
Colours oscillate between Indigo and Vermilion.
Varanasi has no boundaries.

Have you ever thought that Varanasi
has dreamed more dreams than you?
Ocean-depth dreams
clinging on the sealed mouth of the city...
Perhaps, not.
We don't want our minds to be touched.

I was living in a time of straight line
till the historic stones touched me.
My body was hollowed out and unspoken eras took shape—
I walked down the steps and floated a Lotus.

If you care to know, Varanasi teaches you to love,
not to hold but to release.
It melts in the air...
And where ever you are it caresses your cheek
with long-fingered hands.

In the muted tones beneath the summer blaze
the heart is captivated, inhaling the golden breath.
Sadhus, fakhirs, pilgrims wander—
They mirror each other's colour.

In Varanasi if you are a seeker
there is only one hour, no day, no night.
There is only the knowing luminosity
illuminating the endless.

Varanasi takes away my language
They become pungent, like radish bloats...
Reduced to silence, I become aware of the morning droplets
attracting butterfly song.

What made Varanasi survive across millennia
in spite of crumbled empires and kings vanquished?
Again and again it withstood onslaught
for Grace and Benediction are the city's keepers.

Many say all roads end in Varanasi,
but I voice the opposite.
Your eyes bloom like two large Water Lillies
and the world is at your fingertips.

Footfalls, footfalls, footfalls
day and night it reverberate in Varanasi.
Language, letters fall off, wrap around
roots, steps and feet...
I untangle those letters
and preserve them in my note pad.

Proud pillars of Chunar sandstone of Darbhanga ghat
now a display board for graffiti,
fretting like a sick child, it cannot breathe.
Heritage has become an obsolete word.

Fires still smoldering on the ghat
perhaps, a secret conspiracy by Agni.
The western sky red tinged
heralding a day benevolent and narcotic.

When you are inside Viswanath Mandir
your search for god ends in a Linga
seeing for two minutes amid jostling crowd.
But when you come out and strangers smile
you are a temple welcoming and vast.

Despite the sharp wind and the air thick with winter finery,
Dasaswamedh ghat is packed with people for the evening Aarati
each with their own dream-desire...
The lamps glitter against the Indigo Ganga
but the flame touches the blessed few.

Went to Sarnath the other day,
in search of Buddha and Bodhi Brikshya,
instead touched the Stupa like a trusting child.
What remained was my heart throbbing hard...

When I see the pillared balconies with intricate jali work,
forgotten houses with creepers for company,
I make all kinds of movements that release my endorphins
retiring to a seat reserved for daydreaming.

No words, nothing,
only the sun slowly emerging over the horizon
and the Ganga still like rose-gold satin.
I look at my palms where dreams are etched.

When ears are deafened by noise
and eyes blinded by shadowless midday,
just then barren thoughts turn lush
and you become a pilgrim of peace.

You watch paper boats floating on the river near the steps.
If the city had a tongue it could tell you it's story
if it had a voice it could sing all those forgotten melodies.
Now it lies melted and formless
waiting for words from you.

you run barefoot.
You run with your shoes on
you run, run, run...
Suddenly you are standing near the Ganga,
a door to lean, looking at the horizon
where boundaries peter out.

You come to Varanasi and maybe find something you desire
and then there is still a little that evades.
You move forward in darkness.
Varanasi smiles, dazzles your insight with light.

Walking solitary in the narrow lanes
my ears pick up ancient sounds.
Right then I am assailed by the smell of
damp walls and cow dung—
but I will not have it in any other way.

Untie your tress of wisdom Varanasi,
don't hold it with a clasp.
Men misinterpret you, not knowing your ancient insight.
Open your mouth and let words roll out,
lingering to the end of time.

To greet dawn
people throng the ghats.
Few are lucky who perceive darkness
behind the light.

The Shiva Linga is so dark almost a black hole.
The overpowering smell of ghee, milk
flowers, Bael leaves and
you realize your path has almost vanished.

The scholars debate,
the Apsaras sing songs of love,
the sun leaves footprints of light across millennia.
Varanasi's root stretches from oral memory to script.

The Aghoris sit quietly in quiet niches of Varanasi
bare bodied, ash-smeared.
They seem to say, come take my thought-passport
and everything that belong to me...
Just leave a little space so I can embrace you.

Standing beneath a canopy, I watch the river
and the droppings of pigeons on the steps.
The lighted flower lamps afloat—
Each almost an island on the move
speaking wordlessly to you.

The alleys twist and coil up in front of close knit houses,
old, new—a medley of architecture.
There are no sidewalks...
Shadows fall on the pathways like an unknown painting.

The burning ghats have people building pyres.
The bodies would be reduced to ash soon,
floating on the Ganga unwitnessed,
without gender, without a proper name.

The Ganga flows, like a prophet takes everything in.
I go down the steps of the ghat.
On every stone is a Marigold and prayer waiting.

The lanes are so narrow that houses touch each other
and sunlight a filigree design.
But there are messages on every enmeshed overhead wire,
marvels on every bend.

The city waits expectantly for the cool evening breeze
after a hot scorching day.
It arrives like a love letter
long after the hand has turned to ash.

At daybreak, the sun leaps up from the horizon
with a russet duster
wiping the shadows of an infinite city.
Varanasi wakes, stretches itself
before it is engulfed in finitude

The languid summer like a forlorn love lingers
and two little hours stolen.
I lie nailed to the ghat, the umbrella dark—
my body too heavy to rise.

The moon lets the water swell.
The Ganga rises and washes the steps of the ghat.
I sit on the stone slab dipping my feet in the river
letting them be rinsed by waves of warmth.

The river flows with tears of separation and resurrection...
Against a screen of fireflies I become
a mist in the moonlight.

Varanasi is a city with a mystic heart.
Here the gods don't threaten with
Ten Plagues of Egypt—
Rather they come down as you and me
getting dissolved as dust under your feet.

Varanasi is whispering its secrets
to those who want to hear.
I murmur mine to Varanasi, smile,
and then fade into the shadow of a loggia.

Varanasi spreads somber within certain quarters
left alone to nostalgia.
Here it smells of crushed flowers, dhatura and cow dung.
Turn a corner, the smell changes
to Seekh Kebab, Sahi Korma, Gosht Biryani.
Smell to measure a gap.

Some say it is a stone-god
some say it is a Linga.
Some see eyes in the stone, some stars...
Only few find fulfillment.

Smell from small transparent attar vials,
incense sticks and kumkum
house waste, filth and dirt all mingle like
strollers, tourists and pilgrims.
The lanes are narrow, yet ample for those with a flower
inside their heart.

Sitting on the ruined balcony of an old palace
I let the language of night envelop me.
Down below the Ganga flows to unreachable distance.
I try to inhale its memories.

Varanasi is a city of fragments and unfinished stories
yellow street lamps and unsealed dreams.
You rummage through ephemeral tales
and find yourself coated with words.

Cities of the past, sleeping cities, dead cities,
nonexistent cities,
adjectives that adorn Varanasi.
Right now she is afraid,
she can hear the night horses coming.
She is frightened to die once more.

Soon Varanasi will be stories and pictures archived.
The flyovers and multiplexes will make it modern no doubt.
Perhaps, there will be ears
that by some miracle will pick up an ancient echo.
Perhaps, there will be eyes
that will decipher Varanasi from this avant-garde avalanche.

I have a love-hate relationship with you.
I hate the dust and broken roads and
promise never to return.
Just when my thoughts end you hypnotize me,
enigma that you are, Varanasi...

Sharmila Ray is a poet and non-fiction essayist writing in English and featured in India and abroad. She has authored ten poetry books and edited a few collections on Indian Poetry in English, the recent being *Bridging Continents*, a volume of Indo-American poets with Gopal Lahiri. Ray was also an Advisory Board Member (English) with Sahitya Akademi. In addition, she is an Associate Professor of the Department of History at City College, Kolkata. Ray has received many awards for poetry, and her poems have been translated into Urdu, Hindi, Marathi, Bengali, Spanish, Slovene, and Tajik, to name a few.

www.ingramcontent.com/pod-product-compliance
Lightning Source LLC
LaVergne TN
LVHW041129150826
845673LV00007B/2245

* 9 7 8 9 3 9 1 4 3 1 8 0 8 *